# Hacking
# Billable Hours

Elizabeth Miller

**Hacking Billable Hours**

Copyright © 2022 Elizabeth Miller

Front Cover Design Credit: Trace Crisp t@photosbytrace.com

Back Cover: Freddy Solis

Produced by: Anspach Media

ISBN 13: 978-1-7377355-2-6

Printed in USA

**Disclaimer:**

# Dedication

I dedicate this book to my husband and my biggest fan, Richard D. Miller. You have stood by me no matter how far-fetched my goals may have seemed. You have always encouraged me to reach for the sky and never be dissuaded by anyone.

ELIZABETH M. MILLER
Author

*"You win some and you lose some, but you get paid for all of them."*
- Anonymous

*"One thing I disliked about being a lawyer was billing for my time."*
- Andrew Yang

# What People Are Saying

*"This simple, yet highly effective guide, if followed, can help your firm transform from struggling with cash flow problems to being prosperous with eager to pay clients. Elizabeth has laid out the very steps she teaches in her practice to give you, the reader, the very tools needed to hack your billable hours and create a dynamic, profitable business model. I highly recommend you give a copy of this book to everyone in your office, so they understand the importance of billing."* ~ **Rob Anspach**, Anspach Media

*"This book is a perfect crash course for (1) the young lawyer going out on his or her own that needs to know what Elizabeth has been teaching for 30 +years, (2) the small boutique firm that is hiring regularly and whose partners cannot spend a ton of time explaining the concept of billing (because they need to bill!), (3) a lawyer with great experience, but who has struggled his or her entire career with getting their billing woes corrected, or (4) the lawyer that works so hard, however wonders at the end of every month why they are not making more money. The secrets to billing and running a successful law firm are not hidden; they are found throughout this book. Reading this book, and keeping it in the offices of your firm, will be one of the keys to your success!"* ~ **John DeGirolamo,** Founding Partner, In Law We Trust, P.A.

*"As a former Big Law attorney turned business coach and consultant, this book speaks to my heart. I wish I had Hacking Billable Hours early in my legal career to help with the systems and tips necessary to maximize this often-overlooked business function. This practical guide on how to get paid properly and on time is a must-read for attorneys at every stage. I highly recommend this book."* ~ **Jen Grosso**

*"This is by far the go-to guide for billing. If your firm is not using this book, you're doing a disservice to your practice. Elizabeth Miller has proven and provided techniques that work. She is by far the best out there in managing law firms and her hands-on techniques are easy to follow and the most effective. There is no surprise that our office will use this go-to guide for billing. Liz is amazing and works wonders. No surprise - this book is necessary no matter what kind of billing you do."* ~ **Milton Toro Marquez**, Esq - Acevedo Law Firm, LLC

*"As a paralegal/administrator, Liz Miller's methods have assisted me in implementing successful billing procedures for my law firm. It has taught me how to develop and maintain procedures which allow our firm to collect fees and to maintain retainers on account to ensure that the law firm will always be paid. Hacking Billable Hours is a must read for lawyers and non-lawyers because it contains important information, even for clients. Every law firm timekeeper, from partner to legal assistant, needs to read and have at their disposal a copy of this book. It is an easy and informative read with valuable information. Liz Miller is definitely the go-to person when it comes to law office administration. I highly recommend her and this book."* **Brenda Ross**, Paralegal - Florida

*"I've owned my firm for 10 years and I've worked with Liz Miller for the last 2. She is an absolute master at giving law firm owners no-nonsense, actionable advice. This book is right on target. If you have any questions about whether your billing practices are up to snuff, this book will get you there."* **Mike Ziegler** – Partner, Ziegler Diamond Law

*"Hacking Billable Hours is the perfect book for any attorney, paralegal, or other billing member of a law firm that needs a guide or a quick refresher course on proper billing and collections. Billing is important; it is very important. Without billing, lawyers and law firms do not make any money. Yet, it is not taught in law school. Unfortunately, billing is also uncomfortable or is unfamiliar to new members of a law firm. Hacking Billable Hours is the perfect, concise guide that explains billing and collections in easy to understand language. This book provides key examples of how billing should be done, how collections should be handled, and how to ensure your firm is paid for its work. Do not fall into the trap of working for free. Make Hacking Billable Hours a part of your firm's library. You worked for your money. You earned it. Make sure you are paid for it. In Hacking Billable Hours, Elizabeth Miller, and her 30 years of experience, will teach you how."* – **J. Robert Angstadt**, Founding Partner, Tampa Divorce

*"One of the most important things an attorney can do to keep their law firm doors open is to bill properly for their time. My firm has worked with Liz the past 2 years and has benefited greatly from her wealth of knowledge on how to run a successful law practice. Her most recent book really hones in on best billing practices, which can be the difference between a successful law practice and a struggling practice. Highly recommend this book to sharpen your billing skills!"* - **Kaelyn Diamond**, Partner - Diamond Ziegler Law

# Table of Contents

Elizabeth Miller

# Introduction

My hope for this book is to help new lawyers avoid the missteps many lawyers have made in their careers when it comes to getting paid, to help veteran lawyers sharpen their sword when it comes to legal billing and collection of fees, and finally to help educate non-lawyers how to get the biggest bang for their buck. While the state of the law is not static, the goal is to give you a lifeboat, regardless of what kind of billing your firm does, that you can reach for no matter the situation.

So many lawyers have problems with getting their billing out to their clients on any regular basis. I'm not sure why – but – the answers to everything you want to know about billing but were afraid to ask will be in this book.

It's hard to believe that I have spent over 30 years working with the legal profession. I was there when we started with manual typewriters and moved on through to memory typewriters and now computers. I remember using a hand ledger to write both operating and trust account checks, and reconciliations were painstakingly done by hand. Now everything has a computer program, making things faster with less chance for a mistake.

The one thing, however, that has not changed is the need to bill clients. We went from typed bills prepared without a computer program to keeping track of time and being able to enter payments received and trust retainers replenished with case management software. But the one thing about Billing that has not changed is BILLING.

It truly sends chills down my spine to hear a lawyer say, *"I don't have time to do billing"*, or *"I'll get to it as soon as I finish . . ."* with whatever has their attention at the moment. Before you know it another month, or three, have gone by and NO BILLING. No wonder the Billing never gets done – because somehow something else seems more important.

But really, aside from doing the work, what is more important than getting out the billing every month?

There is *nothing* more important than getting out billing. Believe me, the first time your employees don't get paid, or payroll or the rent is late – you will realize just how important billing is to your firm. So, what is the issue with getting billing done?

The very short explanation seems rather simple – do the work, enter a timeslip and at the end of the month send out bills and get paid. Is it really that easy?

The answer is yes!!

It is really that easy. You need to bill regularly. No more of the "this month the client will get a bill and they won't get another one for 3 months". They need to get billed every single month. Every month. Not just when you feel like it or when you need money. *EVERY MONTH*!

This book has broken down billing into manageable tasks with step-by-step instructions whether you are doing hourly billing, flat fee, value billing or hybrid billing.

And YOU don't have to do the billing. Outsourcing billing is not that uncommon these days and it is one less thing your staff has to worry about. And believe me, as my lawyer clients already know, the revenues generated that you will recover will far outweigh any monies that you spend outsourcing billing.

You just have to enter time CONTEMPORANEOUSLY for each client so that the Billing can be sent out every month. Trust transfers can be made, replenishments can be requested, client ledgers updated, and the trust account reconciled. Next month – repeat.

We make it easy! Just follow the rules and you will be amazed at how the money starts coming in. So, let's get down to the nitty gritty and start talking BILLING!!

Elizabeth Miller
*Law Practice Management Consultant*
*And Best-Selling Author*
*From Lawyer to Law Firm*
Tampa, Florida

Elizabeth Miller

# Chapter One

## *What Are Billable Hours?*

Billing is a pivotal component to the financial success of every law practice. With that comes, of course, collections. The firm's billing generates the revenues that comprise the financial foundation of any law practice. The survival of the law firm depends on collection of fees owed to the firm. Without billing, whether it is hourly, flat fee, value or some other hybrid billing, there is no law firm. And this includes cases that fit into the category of "flat fee" cases. Many firms are trying to avoid keeping track of billable hours, and the headaches that come with the collection of those fees by using flat fee retainers, at least initially. Billable hours are any case that is not a contingency.

So, no matter what kind of billing it is, if it is not a contingency case, it is a billable matter.

You can measure the effectiveness of your billing and collection practices with the percentage of receivables that are collected every month. That is, not the client who requires repeated follow-up to collect $200; but clients who send payment in response to an invoice. Generating revenues is about *managing the business of practicing law.*

Nothing strikes a nerve with clients more than having to pay legal fees. Why do clients think it is acceptable for lawyers to work for free? No one asks a doctor for a discount on a bypass or an appendectomy. In fact, it would probably be quite disconcerting if a doctor offered "discounted" surgical procedures.

In today's economy, the client wants to reduce their legal expenses and still receive good service with satisfactory results. This is the "have your cake and eat it too" phenomenon.

Historically, family law cases for example were hourly billable. The client paid an upfront retainer, usually non-refundable, against which the firm billed time. When, in theory, the retainer was down to $500 or $1000, a replenishment would be billed to the client. That replenishment went into trust, and again the firm would bill against the monies held in trust. This is, of course, is where the rub always comes in – getting the client to replenish the retainer.

Family law used to be an area that was almost exclusively billed hourly, especially when it was not an uncontested dissolution. To avoid the issue, some family law lawyers are using a flat fee retainer through mediation after which if the case does not settle at mediation the case is going to trial. At that point, the lawyer and client would sign an hourly retainer agreement and the client would pay a trial retainer agreement to continue to move forward.

This might seem like a good safeguard, at the outset, to have collected a flat fee with a cut-off through a hearing, mediation, or disposition. However, what happens when an unexpected motion needs to be handled or there is some kind of dispute?

Unfortunately, these limited flat fee retainers cannot possibly take all scenarios into account and the law firm could end up doing work for free. If you are doing a flat fee retainer, be sure to provide for hearings that are not part of the "flat fee".

Most clients pay their bills begrudgingly. They know they need a lawyer, and they want the best – they just have trouble paying for it whether it is financial or otherwise. Even if the outcome was favorable or far exceeded their expectations, you will hear the complaints. Get used to it!

Sometimes, the only real money you will see from a client is their initial retainer paid at the commencement of representation. After that, getting paid will be like pulling teeth. Be sure to estimate as accurately as possible what you need to cover the fees for services to be rendered. Get a cost retainer as well – you do not need to be advancing costs on behalf of a client and then trying to get that money back.

Let's face it – money is a touchy subject. No one wants to part with their money, but they want the best representation that money can buy. You need to find a middle ground with clients: not too much so they do not feel like they are being taken advantage of, not too little so that you don't get stuck holding the money bag.

The bottom line is that clients need to pay for your services, and your law firm needs their fees paid to stay in business. It becomes financially counterproductive to bill a client for services rendered and costs incurred and then spend the equivalent of that time trying to get paid.

When you reach the point where the work done and the collection of monies take the same amount of time, your time is actually better spent sitting on the beach.

# Chapter Two

## *Sound Practices To Set Up The Foundation For Effective Legal Billing*

It is rare that a client will ever be totally satisfied with their bills, regardless of the outcome of their case. Call the outcome satisfactory, exceptional, outstanding, or superb. The client will not be happy because they have to pay.

There is a lot to do in law firms. But having billing procedures in place, with rare exception, can make all the difference in generating regular collection of fees from your clients. Following a close second to doing the actual work on the client file is doing the *billing*. If bills are not prepared and sent in such a way that the clients actually pay their bills, then the billable hours mean nothing.

Except, how much time you have invested in a case that you will never get paid for.

The clients that I handle billing for have a more than 95% collection rate and less than 5% accounts receivable. This is because requests for replenishments are timely sent, payment deadlines of 5 days are observed and lawyers do not undertake things like a mediation or deposition without having the funds in their trust account, in advance.

It is important that there are procedures that are followed when it comes to billing. Often, firms will outsource their billing because everyone is too busy generating billable hours. Totally understandable – as long as the billing is sent every single month without fail and all other efforts to collect the monies owed to the firm are followed.

Using effective legal billing, and being very accurate about your billing entries, will give clients less reason to complain. The less reason they have to complain, the more inclined they should be to pay your invoice or request for a replenishment retainer.

Make sure that you keep careful track of the fees and costs retainer paid by a client.

This might sound crazy but hear me out…

If there is an error on the initial funds the client has paid you, the client will not take your bills as being accurate and they will always scrutinize every invoice. When a client takes their time to carefully look over an invoice to the point that they are scrutinizing it for errors, it is never done upon receipt of the bill. They don't get the bill and sit down and look at it. Their thinking is this is an invoice from the lawyer who did not get the retainer right, I need to look at every entry on this bill. Now it could be a week before they look at the bill, it could be sooner, or it could be later.

While this might be a delay tactic, you laid the groundwork by showing that you could not accurately reflect their initial retainer. There is no one to blame but you and the person who does your billing.

When the time that you have billed is at or near the used balance of the retainer agreement, you need to ask that the retainer be replenished. Every time you ask for a retainer to be replenished, because of the amount, this will send the client to look over your invoices and make sure everything is accurate.

Hopefully you were specific enough in your retainer agreement (we will get to that later in this book) to give the client a reasonable amount of time – *5 days* – to replenish the retainer.

After the 5 days have expired, you will want to follow up with the client to get those additional funds so you can keep working the case. Keeping track of retainers and making sure there is sufficient time before the original retainer runs out will always ensure that you are working for money.

Time entries on legal billing software need to be entered CONTEMPORANEOUSLY. There is no reason that time cannot be entered contemporaneously. Do you remember what you had for breakfast last week, or even yesterday? Odds are that you probably don't remember. I know I don't. So, if you can't remember what you had for breakfast, how do you know that you will capture every SECOND of billable time on a case?

The answer – you can't! There is no one – NO ONE – who can convince me that they remember every single thing they did from memory within the last 30 days and remember to bill for it. Not to mention what a waste of time it is to now sit down and try to reconstruct the billing for the past month!

Contemporaneously billing means that you keep your billing program open and bill for every file that you work on. Even at 6 hours per day (we will allow 2 hours for unaccountable time), that is 120 hours per month. Once you have mastered the art of contemporaneously billing, you may well find that you can actually bill 8 hours per day just because you have become so efficient at billing.

Remember, clients are not as impressed by the number of billable hours that you worked on their case, or that you achieved a more than satisfactory outcome for them. To the client, you always spent too much time, and you could have done better in less time.

The number of billable hours only means how much you are charging them. No matter what, the numbers of hours will always be too many.

Make sure you or the person who does your billing reviews billing entries every week. This is when you can catch errors such as grammar or spelling and then make appropriate revisions. You can save this for the end of the month, but you will not want to hold up the billing process.

If you see a timekeeper making an error, using poor language, being too wordy or doing block billing, the time to catch it is now. You don't want to look at and revise an entire month of billing entries when it is time to send out bills. This will delay the entire process – and it's important to get your bills out at the same time every month. When your billing becomes erratic, you can expect your collections to become erratic as well. It is important that you stick with a schedule that the client can depend on.

In its simplest form, the billing cycle should go like this:

1.     Establish a regular billing cycle every 30 days. And then do it! Tell the client and *put it in the retainer agreement* that the client will receive a billing statement every month.

2.     Cut off time for the month is the last day of the month at 5 pm. This could vary depending on what your thirty-day billing schedule is. Because every timekeeper should be entering their time contemporaneously, the time entries should be ready to go at 5 pm. If you insist on consistency, your staff will know every month what the cut-off and they will work with it. Run your pre-bills at 5 pm that day.

3.     Go over grammatical and spelling errors and look for other inconsistencies which are obvious. This is really another once over and if you have been reviewing billing entries every week, this won't take long at all.

4.     The pre-bills are then circulated to the partner(s) who is responsible for the case and should be returned by the 3$^{rd}$ day.

5.     If everyone is timely in meeting deadlines to return the edited pre-bills, the actual bills, edited and revised, can go to the client on the 5$^{th}$ day of the billing cycle.

Of primary importance is the continuity and consistency of billing procedures. It does not matter what dates you choose to do pre-bills and send the final bills to clients. What matters is the consistency of sending bills every month, *at the same time*, so clients will know when to expect them – and pay them!

This is the reason that your mortgage and car payments are due on the same day every month. You know when the bills are due, and you plan accordingly. It helps your clients to know what to expect so they can budget their finances and, in turn, will help your firm collect its revenues on a more consistent basis.

You can bill your client at the end of every month, in the middle of the month or twice a month. It does not really matter what the procedure is in terms of when you do the billing. The bottom line here is to adhere to a regular billing schedule with no exceptions. This way a client knows when their bills will be presented and need to be paid, and you have taken away the excuses for a client to be late with their payment.

# Chapter Three

## *Hourly Rates*

Hourly rates are a tricky issue. Charge too much and you will significantly reduce your client base, and the clients you do have will expect everything from you. This will likely include receiving calls, text messages and emails on weekends.

Charge too little and you may have 1) more clients but you are working for less money and having to make up the difference in volume or 2) not enough clients because people will wonder why your fees are so low. This, of course, means working a lot harder to make the same amount of money.

As a young lawyer, hourly fee rates are usually somewhere between $250 and $295 per hour. This seems a reasonable rate and it won't keep you working 24/7 just to keep 50 cents of every dollar that you bill.

As you get closer to the 5 to 7-year mark, you can start inching up your fees probably by about $50 to $100 per hour. Remember though, raising your rates means notifying your clients thirty (30) days in advance that you intend to raise your fees.

Often what firms do when they decide to raise their fees is to allow the current clients to be billed at the rate they agreed to when they signed the retainer. New clients whose cases were taken on after the firm increased their rates will be billed at the new rate.

Lawyers fear that current clients whose hourly rates are increased may seek counsel elsewhere because of the increase. For the most part, they are probably right.

After 10 years, it is not uncommon for lawyers to charge as much as $375 to $450 an hour for their time even if they are not board certified. There is something about experience that you cannot substitute with a board certification.

In many firms, clients pay for associates, paralegals and other staff members time working on their cases. A paralegal with a good solid 10 years of experience can charge between $125 and $175 per hour. Oftentimes, the paralegal is used to do less intense document preparation or other services that would cost the client twice that amount if the lawyer or associate were to do it. The legal assistant, also, bills for their time and those rates are usually $75 to $125 per hour, depending on the extent of their experience and the type of work they are doing.

In an hourly billable firm, every person that touches the file is a timekeeper. It is important, then, to note that work assignments are given on a "most competent, least expensive person" to accomplish the task. This is fair to the client and also fair to the firm. It doesn't make sense for the paralegal to be confirming mediations, appointments, etc. with a client when the legal assistant is capable of doing that. And it doesn't make sense for an associate lawyer to be copying pleadings to put together a trial notebook when the paralegal is capable of doing that.

One-hundred and twenty hours (120) hours to one-hundred and thirty (130) hours per month seems like a fair billing quota for all timekeepers. Some firms hold lawyers to a higher standard but oftentimes that just means there is less care taken with handling matters because the lawyers are in a rush to move onto the next thing to get their billable hours in.

Using 120 hours per month, this is what a 4-person firm's billing should look like every month:

Partner $48,000                    ($400/hour – 120 hours)
Associate $39,000                  ($325/hour – 120 hours)
Paralegal $18,000                  ($150/hour – 120 hours)
Legal Assistant $12,000            ($100/hour – 120 hours)

**Total Monthly Billables:**              **$117,000.00**

Now, wouldn't it be great if every month's billables looked like this?

Yeah, sure it would.

But the reality is that no one's billables look like this every month. There are trials that will increase your monthly billings, and there are slow months that will reduce your monthly billings, or people who go on vacation for a week. This is why it is important that *every billable hour is accounted for*.

We used to use the business model of 3's – one third to salary, one third to overhead, one third to profit.

Ah, but if things only worked that way! This is why capturing every billable minute is important. This is why doing billing *non-contemporaneously* is not going to work. Every minute spent working on a file needs to be accounted for. It is the only way to make sure that your law firm recovers all the fees that are due every month for billable time.

The only one that benefits from doing a poor job billing and collecting is your *clients*!

# Chapter Four

## *Retainer Agreements – What You Need To Know*

Funny thing about retainer agreements – if it isn't in writing, it never happened!

Retainer agreements are meant to protect the lawyer and the client. Everything that a firm agrees to do needs to be reduced in writing in the retainer agreement and signed by both parties. Be sure to give the client a copy of the retainer agreement and have them sign that they received a copy.

From the amount of the fee, what will be done for the fee, what the hourly rates are and the billing and collection practices -- it all needs to be included. There is *nothing* more important than the retainer agreement. So, let's address each section of the retainer agreement and see how you need to make sure your firm is protected.

Whether you are working on an hourly retainer or a flat fee, the retainer agreement needs to reflect the retainer amount. On a flat fee case, it's simple. The flat fee is paid upfront, and the retainer is signed. On an hourly rate, the retainer needs to be reflected on the agreement and work should *never* begin without the retainer being paid in full.

Now, if you choose to take a partial retainer and believe that your client will pay the rest, great! I hope that works out for you. But experience has shown us that it does not always work out, and once that retainer is signed, you are in until the Court says you are out.

Retainers whether flat fee or hourly, are usually non-refundable. This means they can go into the operating account. Time is billed against the non-refundable retainer even though it is non-refundable. Billable time is tracked and when the initial retainer is down to $500 or $1000, it is time to send a retainer replenishment request. Usually a payment deadline of five (5) days is included. If you do not include a payment deadline in your retainer agreement, you will be chasing down payments. Having $500 or $1000 gives you enough time to file a motion to withdraw if the client does not pay the replenishment.

*Remember, if it isn't written in the retainer agreement – it never happened!*

When there is a dispute with a retainer agreement and either the Court or the Bar association is called in to settle the dispute, they will usually rule in favor of the client when it comes to ambiguity of the retainer agreement. It is presumed that the lawyer should have known better since they drafted the agreement, and the client was innocent.

The replenishment retainer, unlike the initial non-refundable retainer, needs to go into trust. In order to move that money out of trust, a bill needs to be presented to the client. Another reason why billing is so important – you can't move that money unless your firm has earned it. And you cannot prove that you earned it *unless you have billed for it*.

Several years ago, I worked for a very short period for a lawyer who would move money from trust when the operating account got low. In an abundance of caution, I asked what files the money was being moved for. The response was "no files".

See, it turned out that what the lawyer wanted to do was move $10,000 from trust to operating, and at the end of the month when billing was done, they would deduct that $10,000 from the total monies that we needed to be moved.

The Bar association has a problem with that – a BIG problem – and so do I.

What I tried to get the lawyer to do was generate bills so we could move money. But she said that would have been too time consuming and the other way was better. It really wasn't better, what it really was – just faster.

I did not even last a month there; I was not getting into trouble for moving client's money out of trust with no invoice.

Your retainer agreement needs to address the following items:

       a) Amount of retainer to be paid. Be sure to include everywhere possible, "non-refundable" or "deemed earned upon receipt".

b) Services to be provided – flat fee, value billing, hourly or contingency. Be specific. If this is a family law case be sure to include up to what point the services are engaged. For example, "dissolution of marriage through mediation". Once mediation has occurred, if the client wants you to continue to represent them, you need to sign a new retainer. It is very important to be specific.

c) Set forth the hourly rates for all the timekeepers who work for the firm. If the client has a question, everyone will go back to the retainer agreement. Make sure the hourly rates are all in there.

d) The cost retainer is separate from the fee retainer. Never pay the costs (filing fees, process server) out of the fee retainer. It makes it much cleaner to get a separate cost retainer from the client at the beginning of the case. If there are left over costs at the conclusion of the case, they can be applied to a fee balance or returned to the client at the conclusion of the case.

e) Be specific about billing. Billing will occur every 30 days. The initial retainer is non-refundable. Replenishment retainers will go into trust and the firm will bill against the amount in trust. Payment is due within five (5) days of the date of the invoice. If no payment is received, lawyer may file a motion to withdraw.

f) Replenishment fee retainers should be requested when there is $1000 left on retainer. A replenishment fee request needs to go out to the client and the retainer agreement needs to include a deadline of five (5) days to pay up. Again, if you do not include deadlines, the client has no point of reference.

g) Include in the retainer that if the firm needs to pursue the client by filing suit for unpaid fees or costs, what county suit will be filed in. Be sure to include that the judgment for fees will be recorded against any property owned by the client. In this way, if a piece of real estate needs to be sold, you will be sure to get paid what you are owed.

h) If a client has a mediation, deposition or hearing coming up, and there is not enough money to cover whatever is that is scheduled, get a replenishment on the retainer. You do not want to be stuck holding the money bag, especially if the mediation or deposition does not go well or as well as the client wanted.

By the time you need to ask for a replenishment retainer, you generally have a good sense of where this case is going. You know who is on the other side by now, and dare I say, you know if he/she will be a jerk or if he/she will be reasonable. You know what the opposing party will be like, and you likely know who the Judge will be.

Take all those things into consideration, as well as the financial health of your client, and you can come up with an amount for a replenishment retainer. Ask for too little and you will be requesting a replenishment every two months, or more. You do not want to make it seem like you are always asking for money.

There are some instances, in a family law case for example, where you will have a client (usually the wife) come to you and tell you that the husband is the bread winner and controls all the finances. These cases are sometimes a slippery slope, and you want to be careful.

In this instance, do your due diligence. Before signing on this client who will want you to get your fees from the husband, make sure it is what has been represented to you before you get involved. Check out the story. See if the husband is the bread winner and that it is reasonable to pursue the husband for fees. If the information is accurate, then by all means, take on that client.

The bottom line is to make sure that the retainer agreement, and everything associated with your representation of an hourly client, is put into writing. Make sure there are no ambiguities that can come back later on to bite you. There is nothing worse than giving a case everything that you have, only to be short-changed in the end and holding that money bag.

# Chapter Five

## *It's a Trap!!*
## *Common Missteps In Legal Billing*

Clients can be really funny when it comes to billing. There are so many things that will set a client off, or, at least give them reason to ask questions about their bill, which in their mind means that they can delay payment of that bill.

You know that if a client has just one question about their bill, that, in their mind, justifies them not paying the entire bill until that question is answered. That is one reason that it is very important when a client calls with a billing question that someone, preferably the person who handles the billing, gets that message, and calls them back as soon as possible.

The work that you do for clients' needs to be above reproach. No typos, no misspellings, no misstatements of the facts, all the dates accurate. So, too, your billing should be perfect! First, it gives your client a lot less to complain about. But, also, if you cannot get your bills right, how does the client know everything else you do on their case is right? They don't! There are a number of things that we need to watch out for when we send bills to a client.

*Not billing enough hurts the firm.*

Take, for example, this time entry for a .2 of time entered:

Telephone call to JA to secure dates and times for proposed hearing; contact opposing counsel to coordinate date and time for hearing; call back to JA to confirm date and time of hearing; prepare Notice of Hearing; e-file and e-serve via court portal; send to client.

In what world does it take 12 minutes to do all of this? Have you ever tried to get through to a JA before? Have you ever called opposing counsel and cleared a date that quickly? Then called back the JA, prepared a Notice of Hearing, served it through the portal and then sent a copy to your client? Never.

But here comes the rub. This would probably be a .8 or a .9 of billable time. But if you block bill this altogether, the client will zero right in on the 0.9 and the complaints will start. Better to bill this entry this way:

Telephone call to JA to get dates and times to coordinate hearing                .2

Telephone call to opposing counsel to coordinate date and time for hearing                .2

Prepared Notice of Hearing and e-filed/e-served via court e-portal                .3

Emailed Notice of Hearing to client
                .2

This billing is still the 0.9, but in such a way that it is acceptable to the client and does not raise any eyebrows.

This billing entry will likely not give the client a reason to call and complain. Not that they should, because the services and charges were legitimate.

Be careful when you send out bills. Make sure the person who does your billing pays close attention and that time entries are not duplicated. This usually happens when someone is trying to recollect what they did on files weeks ago rather than entering time *contemporaneously*. When time entries are double billed, you can be very sure that your client will catch it. When they do, it will give them a reason to re-check the entire bill again. Another delay.

There are some things that you just cannot bill a client. For example, an associate is working on their case, and the associate leaves. A new associate coming into the firm needs to review the file to be brought up to speed on what is going on. Does the associate bill for their time getting to know the file so they can move forward?

Of course, they should not. But you will want to bill that time and show it as *no charge*. Clients LOVE to see "no charge" on their bills. It goes a long way with clients and really for something like this they should not be charged.

Similarly, if an associate has an office conference with the partner to discuss strategy should the client be billed for both associate and lawyer time? Of course not. The partner and the associate each bill for the time; the associate's time is marked *no charge*. In this way, the higher billing lawyer (partner) time is billed, and the client sees that they are getting the associate for free. Again, clients like to see these entries.

All timekeepers need to be careful to not overcharge for their work. The person who does the billing has a good feel for what is involved in handling legal matters. When I do for my clients, I know how long things will take and if someone billed .2 to draft a motion, I know there is a problem.

In a family law case, for example, when you have a timekeeper, who charges 5.0 hours one day to do mandatory disclosure, then 3.5 hours the following day and then another 3.0 hours – something is wrong here. Furthermore, the time needs to be billed in such a way that it shows a continuation of the project, new records that were being reviewed, revisions and the like:

Reviewed documents for mandatory disclosure to see what documents were produced and see what is missing
1.5

Begin preparing certificate of mandatory with itemized document lists                4.3

Continue preparing mandatory disclosure documents; emailed client regarding question concerning investment account                2.5

Finalize draft of mandatory disclosure for lawyer review                                    2.3

Finally, do not charge a client for the time it takes a staff member to take a payment. Really? The client is paying their bill and there will be a 0.2 on the invoice for someone taking their payment? I get it – keep track of the time. Do it with an entry and mark the time "no charge".

The likelihood of the client having something to complain about the way these time entries are written is almost non-existent.

If you want to get your bills paid timely without any delays, give your clients no reason to complain about their bill. This will certainly speed up the paying process.

Elizabeth Miller

# Chapter Six

## *Pre-Billing: Would You Hire You*

You get a resume from someone who has applied for a job with your organization. You scrutinize the resume and find one typo. Then you find another. You stop looking then throw the resume in the trash. Why?

What does it tell you about the impression that the person is making with the typos in their own resume? Does it give you cause for concern that if they couldn't send out *their own* resume without a typo, what kind of work will they do for you?

Yeah – that's the problem here. So, what does it tell a client when they receive an invoice from you with the client's name spelled wrong, a time entry from another case, a 25-hour charge to review something which should have been 0.25?

It pretty much tells the client the same thing you thought when you got that resume – you don't care about the work product that goes out in your own name. And in the client's mind, you probably don't care much about the work you are doing for the client.

Be sure that your bills are accurate and above reproach. Let your client know that you take pride in your work, even if it is just to bill them for the work you have done.

1. Be sure your billing statement looks professional. The name of the firm, the date, and the correct client matter.

2. Make sure all your descriptions are complete sentences and that there are no abbreviations. A client does not know that a "MTC" is a motion to compel, or that a "NTD" is a notice of taking deposition. The client is paying for your work – and that includes the billing statements every month. Make it something they can read and understand without needing a book on legal abbreviations or explanations of legal terminology.

3. Please make sure the grammar and spelling are correct. There is nothing worse than a bill going out with a typographical (remember that resume??) or a grammatical error. There is simply no excuse for this.

4. Since there is often the chance that your bills may be produced to the other side such as a motion to award lawyers' fees, please make sure to the extent that you can that there is no confidential information or work product contained in a time entry. You can do this when you are doing the bill to send to the client by not being specific about your legal strategy.

The fewer reasons the client has to complain or ask questions about their bill, the less reason there will be to delay payment.

# Chapter Seven

## *Billing Cycles*

The quickest way to get paid. Send a bill.

The quickest way to have a client ask, "what happened to my money"? Don't send a bill for 3 to 6 months, or more. Then send a bill. Watch how fast the client asks, *"what happened to my money?"*.

Believe me – when I take on a lawyer client whose billing has been hit or miss, this has happened to me. I mean, after all, you really can't blame them. One minute, things are going along great, and they assume there is no problem because they haven't gotten a bill. Next day they get a bill and, not only is their retainer used up, but they also owe several thousands of dollars. Yeah – that will get you an upset client wanting to know what happened to their money and why they didn't get a bill sooner.

Your retainer agreement needs to contain language that a bill will be sent every month. This is to let the client know what you and your staff have been working, what you've been working on, how much money has been spent – and – how much is left. If you do not send out a billing statement every month, then you will have to deal with all the questions that will follow when a client gets a bill for 3 or 6 months, or more.

Getting billing statements out does not require any guess work, nor should it require everyone scrambling around in the last-minute begging for more time because they haven't entered time all month.

This will hold up your billing cycle and it should not happen.

Remember, keeping track of time is part of a timekeeper's job. It is not a request. Timekeepers are not doing the firm any favors by not keeping track of their time. It is part of their job. When clients don't pay their bills because they aren't being billed, and there is suddenly no money to pay timekeepers – what then?

Again, *keeping track of time and billing it is part of a timekeeper's job.*

While some firms have incentive programs for their employees who bill over a certain amount, the basic billable quota, usually around 120 hours, is expected as part of the job. You can have the best legal assistant or paralegal working for you, but if they don't bill their time because they are busy doing "work", there's something wrong.

Assuming that the timekeepers have all entered their time contemporaneously, on or about the 25th of the month an email is sent out letting people know that pre-bills will be run on the last day of the month at 5:00 p.m. This gives anyone who has an issue with getting time in to let you know.

After the prebills are done, the billing person reviews all the billing for spelling and typographical errors and any other errors such as block billing or double billing.

The prebills are given to the lawyer(s) to review and make additions, changes and/or deletions. The pre-bills are due back to the billing person by the close of business on the 3rd.

Once received back, all the final changes are made. The final bills are run and emailed to clients or mailed to those without email addresses. This all happens by no later than the 5th day of the billing month, every month, depending on where the weekend falls.

Monies are transferred from trust to operating for the clients who had monies in trust. Entries are made showing trust monies were transferred. The trust account is updated and then reconciled.

The checkbook balance, the bank balance and each client's trust ledger should all have the same balances after trust transfers are made. The trust ledger is then updated for that month. If something is not adding up, that is one of the balances do not match, now is the time to find it.

Now is also the time to send out fee retainer replenishment requests to those clients whose trust balances are under $1,000.00. This needs a tight 5-day follow up. If the trust replenishments are not paid, a follow up phone call needs to be made to the client.

After no payment, the file needs to be brought to the attention of the lawyer to make the decision whether to continue working on the case or to withdraw.

# Chapter Eight

## *Flat Fee/Value Billing Cases*

Many lawyers have chosen to do flat fee or value billing rather than hourly. I believe this, more likely, stems from the billing and collections that need to be done every month. Some lawyers do not like hourly billing because they feel that it encourages doing things less efficiently.

If you take hourly billing out of the equation (most) clients do not care if it takes you three hours or thirty minutes to complete a matter. They want it, and as importantly, done correctly.

When you present your client with a fixed fee matter, you are giving then value for their case and the work they provide. Of course, the number of hours goes into calculating your value, but the client sees the matter in terms of a set value, not how many hours you spend on it.

Flat fee billing and value billing are not the same. Flat fee billing can be value based, but it does not have to be. True value billing is independent on the amount of time the work takes but rather focuses on the actual value of the service to the client. That is, the fees in value billing are based on the "value" to the client, not how long it takes the lawyer times a certain hourly rate equals the fee.

Doing flat fee or value billing means that the lawyer needs to streamline their practice to make it more efficient and to create features that a client is willing to pay for.

I caution lawyers who want to do flat fee billing that every conceivable possibility needs to be covered in that flat fee.

For example, you can do a flat fee on a landlord/tenant evictions with the exception of the hearing. You can include in the retainer that if you need to attend a hearing what the additional fee will be.

For my lawyers who want to do family law cases on a flat fee, they will do a case through mediation for a specific fee. If the case impasses at mediation, the flat fee retainer states that a new hourly retainer needs to be signed with a new retainer fee. In that flat fee retainer, exceptions can be made to attend hearings, etc. The flat fee is set based upon the amount of work that is involved.

Knowing this will only come from experience.

As I said earlier, whatever the agreement is, it needs to be in writing. If it is not in writing, it did not happen.

*Please check your State Bar rules because, although you are billing a client a flat fee, many Bar rules *require* that the attorney track their time. Many lawyers prefer to go flat fee because they feel it avoids the need to keep time records of the work done. If your State Bar requires that you must keep track of your billing, then trying to use a flat fee to avoid keeping track of bill does not accomplish that goal.

# Chapter Nine

## *Trust Accounting -OR-*
## *How To Get In Trouble With The Bar Fast*

Trust account . . . an account maintained with client monies intended to be used for the benefit of the client.

I have had the opportunity to attend four trust account audits. While it was not a pleasant experience, you learn everything you always wanted to know about trust accounting but were afraid to ask.

My experience with trust accounts is the vast majority of lawyers are honest and do not steal their client's money. Most trust accounting problems are merely the result of errors, such as transposition errors, or not being aware that the rules are different for the trust account than they are for just regular accounting processes.

The good news is that case management software means you enter the information into the system once. If you make an error, it is the same error everywhere.

Don't make reconciling the trust account harder than it has to be. If you do it at the end of every billing period (monthly) using the reports generated by your case management software, this should be smooth sailing every month – no matter how much you use your trust account.

Here are some of the pitfalls to watch out for:

- You cannot draw on monies deposited until they clear the bank. Don't draw on trust account monies just deposited thinking there are other client funds in the trust account to cover a check or transfer until a deposit clears. The bar would see that as being "out of trust" for however long it takes for those funds to clear. If you need to draw on funds right away, make sure the deposit is in the form of a bank check or an electronic transfer to deposit. Verify with the bank that the funds are clear *before* you draw on them. It does not matter what the client's sense of urgency is, if the money has not cleared your account, do not draw on it.

- Maintain a ledger for each client that shows every deposit and withdrawal made on behalf of that client. If you use case management software, you can print out a report at the end of the month that will show you every trust accounting activity. If they are set up correctly, you can input information one time and it is reflected on the ledger, on the balance sheet and on the register.

- Reconcile your trust account every month – not just the bank statement. You need to reconcile the bank statement with your client ledgers and your check register every month and make sure all the balances match exactly. When (and if) the Bar ever audits your trust account, they will be looking for a 3-way reconciliation. If all your accounting processes are in order, reconciling the trust account does not take long at all.

- If you take credit cards, please be sure that payments on invoices go into operating and replenishment retainers go into trust.

- If you take retainers that are refundable, the unused proceeds are to be returned to the client at the conclusion of the matter. Make sure that when you take fees from a trust retainer, you have a statement for services rendered reflecting what your firm has earned. You will need this accounting detail if you ever get audited. You cannot just pay your firm fees out of trust without accounting for the client's money.

- A non-refundable retainer does not have to be deposited into trust, however, make sure that your retainer agreement specifically states "non-refundable", "deemed earned upon receipt" and that any "unused funds will not be returned".

- Be sure to include in your retainer agreement that the client agrees that you are permitted to pay the firm out of the fee retainer in trust for any statements for services that are generated. If you do not have a client's permission to move the money, get it before you withdraw money and pay your firm. Make it part of your retainer agreement and you will not have to worry about it.

While the trust account regulations are designed to protect the client from misuse of their funds, even in the case of a bookkeeping mistake such as the transposition of a number, the Bar has little sympathy for error.

Make sure whomever handles your trust account for your firm and does the monthly reconciliations is familiar with all that is involved in preparing a reconciliation that aligns with the Bar rules.

A technicality will usually not result in a reprimand or disbarment. The outcome of a technical trust violation may result in having to hire an accountant to audit and reconcile your trust account every month and submit it to the auditor at the bar for however long the bar decides. No matter what the outcome, a trust account audit really is a headache and an expense and usually a mistake that could have been avoided.

# Chapter Ten

## *Collections From Clients*

Ah, if there were some magical way to collect from clients . . . but there is none!

This is why regular billing every month is so important. If a client won't or can't pay, I'd rather find out after one month than after three to six months. You can incur a lot of fees in three or six months that you won't get paid for.

When you send a client a regular monthly billing statement, the payment is due in five (5) days. When the five days have expired, it's time to get on the telephone and get paid.

Sometimes clients do have a good excuse for not paying. They didn't get the invoice – offer to send a new one and tell them you will call back tomorrow to get payment.

They reviewed the bill but forgot to pay it. Offer to take the payment from them right there on the phone.

The bill was more than they expected, and they cannot pay the whole thing. Ask how much they can afford to pay and offer to take the payment right then. Then ask how they would like to pay the balance and send a promissory note.

At this point do whatever you need to do to get a payment from them and a promise to pay the balance that is due.

Remember, if you can get money from the client, get whatever you can from them.

When the situation turns ugly, and sometimes it will, it is time to protect the firm. If the type of case permits, immediately file a charging lien in the case. If the client has real property (even if it's jointly held with someone else) record the charging lien against the property.

If the case is essentially over and you are trying to collect your fees, I do not recommend hiring a collection agency.

Have your billing person reach out and work out an agreement. Collection agencies charge thirty or forty percent and often settle for less than what is owed. You can offer a thirty or forty percent reduction on the bill and still come out with more money than if you hired a collection agency. If you are inclined to hire someone out of the firm to do the collections, I would recommend a law firm that does collection work as opposed to a collection agency.

But remember, if you follow the step-by-step billing protocols in this book you, like my lawyer clients, should not have a problem with huge accounts receivable.

# Chapter Eleven

## *You As The Client – Duties And Responsibilities*

Remember that saying in real estate - there are 3 important things when looking for real estate: location, location, location!

Well, in hiring a lawyer there are also 3 important things: *get it in writing, get it in writing, get it in writing.* If it isn't reduced to writing, it didn't happen!

The retainer agreement will rule the lawyer/client relationship. It is your responsibility as a client to reduce to writing your agreement concerning payment and cooperation with your lawyer. In it, your lawyer agrees to provide a specific service all in your best interests. Make sure that the following is contained in the agreement so that both of you are protected:

1. The amount of the retainer needs to be specified.

2. The hourly rate of every timekeeper in the office needs to be set forth right in the agreement.

3. The cost deposit needs to be specified. In addition, any cost monies left after a case is over need to be returned to you as the

client, unless there is a balance owed the firm for fees.

4. The services to be rendered need to be set forth in the agreement. For example, in a divorce case, it is possible that you are retaining the law firm to represent you through the conclusion of mediation. Be sure the services rendered are specifically set forth in the contract.

5. If the law firm is only representing you through the conclusion of mediation, a new retainer will have to be prepared once mediation is over and the case has not settled.

6. Your lawyer needs to send you a billing statement every single month. It should set forth who worked on the file, what they did, how much they charged and at the end of the bill, the total funds you still have remaining on account. Even though it is not your responsibility to chase down your bill, if you don't get a bill the first full month after retaining the lawyer, call up and ask where it is. The last thing you want is a bill 3 months down the road showing that all the funds have been used up and the lawyer wants/needs more money. With a statement every month you

can keep track of your money and plan when you must pay a new retainer.

Remember, if it isn't reduced to writing it never happened. Keep a copy of your retainer agreement handy in case there are ever any questions about what your representation agreement with the lawyer.

Be sure to promptly comply with your lawyer's requests. Clients run up bills oftentimes because a lawyer or their paralegal needs to repeatedly ask for documents, information, witnesses, etc. I have several firms that I do their monthly billing and I see the time entries:

*"Follow up telephone call/email to client to request mandatory disclosure documents again"*.

This time is reflected on your bill by the timekeeper making the request both for purposes of billing and to show that they had to ask for something over and over again.

The quickest way to avoid being charged for repeated requests for compliance is to 1) acknowledge the request, 2) comply with the request be it for information or to confirm time for a deposition, mediation, etc., and 3) if you need time to get some documentation or information for the lawyer, tell them you are working on it and will have it as soon as possible. Give them an approximate time frame so they know how long it will take. Lawyers and their staff make it their business to make sure you keep up with their requests – do not give them a reason to repeatedly bill for requests for the same item or information.

When you are the client who hires a lawyer to represent you in connection with any legal matter, it is as much your responsibility to work with the lawyer as it is the lawyer's responsibility to represent you zealously. To do that, you need to cooperate with the lawyer and always be ready to provide whatever is needed for the lawyer to represent your interests.

Do your best to always cooperate and keep the costs down!

# Chapter Twelve

## *Conclusion*

Billing is a very important law firm function. The purpose of this book is not to overwhelm your law firm with one more thing to do, but to help facilitate this important part of managing the business of practicing law.

Many firms are turning to flat fee or value billing, and that is perfectly okay provided that the fee schedules are such that the firm does not do work that they will not get paid for. The key here is to understand that without the billing component, law firms cannot survive.

The billing protocols set forth in this book, no matter what kind of fee arrangement it is, are not complex. But they are designed for regular monthly billing that will generate regular monthly cashflow for the firm. Consider these protocols a living document that you are constantly building and reinventing as your legal team grows and changes.

Elizabeth Miller

# About The Author

Liz Miller has been working as a Law Practice Management Consultant since 2015 and has over 30 years of experience working with lawyers. She began her career in New York City as a legal secretary in January 1979.

Two years later she obtained her paralegal certification from the Paralegal Institute of New York. In 1985, she moved to Tampa, Florida where she continued with her career until 1988 when she opened Paralegal Professionals. She worked as an independent paralegal for lawyers specializing in plaintiff's personal injury work and medical malpractice.

In 1997, Liz segued her career into law office administrator. She obtained her Bachelor's Degree in Business Administration and then pursued her Master's Degree in Business Administration with a specialty in finance. Through a series of career transitions, Liz opened *From Lawyer to Law Firm* in 2015, helping lawyers with the administration of their law firms including billing.

Liz's last book, *From Lawyer to Law Firm – How to Manage a Successful Law Business,* was published in May 2017 and was #4 on the Best Seller List two weeks after it was published. This book can be purchased on Liz's website at www.fromlawyertolawfirm.com

Liz Miller is a member of the editorial advisory board of *Law Office Manager* magazine. She writes/blogs for the magazine and has also done several webinars including one on Billing/Collections and one on Trust Accounting.

Her professional affiliations include the Hillsborough Bar Association, The Solo and Small Firm Practitioner Section of the HCBA, and the Society of Human Resource Managers.

Liz believes that lawyers sacrifice billable hours when they handle administrative functions. Most law firms do not need a full-time administrator. Liz helps lawyers focus their time and energy on practicing law and taking care of their clients and the lawyer/client relationship, while she takes care of managing the business of practicing law.

Liz Miller can be reached at 813-340-9569 or via email at liz.managementconsultant@gmail.com.

# Check out Liz's website at:
## www.fromlawyertolawfirm.com

**And connect with her on these social platforms:**

**Facebook**
https://www.facebook.com/lawfirmadmin

**LinkedIn**
https://www.linkedin.com/company/from-lawyer-to-law-firm/

www.ingramcontent.com/pod-product-compliance
Lightning Source LLC
Chambersburg PA
CBHW050531210326
41520CB00012B/2524